Start Strong: A four week devotional exploring friends, choices, bullying & conflict.

Published by: Nistel Press

All Scripture quotations, unless otherwise noted, are taken from the Holy Bible, English Standard Version, ESV

Get more information at strongseriesdevos.com.

ISBN: 979-8-9921846-0-0

Printed in USA
Second Edition 2024

a four week devotional for preteens exploring friends, choices, bullying & conflict.

by Joshua Celestin

endorsements

"I wish I knew it's okay to grow away from friends."
- 5th Grade Girl

"I wish I knew how to make friends."
- 4th Grade Boy

"I wish I knew what to do when someone bullied me."
- 5th Grade Girl

"I wish I knew friends can be fake."
- 4th Grade Girl

"I wish I knew what choices to make."
- 4th Grade Girl

"I wish I knew just to be myself. There's nothing to worry about."
- 5th Grade Girl

"I wish I knew to stay away from bad people."
- 5th Grade Boy

"I wish I knew not to be afraid. Do something to stand out."
- 5th Grade Boy

foreword *(for adults)*

With years of experience as a children's pastor and a father, I have come to understand one undeniable truth: childhood is challenging.

Today's generation faces unprecedented influences—from technology and social media to the entertainment industry. These forces constantly vie for their attention, presenting them with more choices than any previous generation during their formative years. This is particularly true for preteens, a group I believe is at their most crucial developmental stage.

As parents, one of the most valuable skills we can equip our children with is the ability to make wise, God-honoring choices. After all, the decisions people make ultimately shape their lives, and this is never truer than during the preteen years. Friends increasingly become a dominant influence in our children's lives, making it essential for preteens to learn the art of choosing their friendships wisely.

"Start Strong" delves into these crucial topics, offering preteens insights and strategies to make prudent decisions and understand the importance of nurturing positive friendships. It is easier to prepare our kids than repair them later, and this book will help you do just that. "Start Strong" is an invaluable resource for initiating this preparatory process, setting the stage for a smoother transition into middle school.

- Heath Bryant, First Orlando KIDS Pastor

START HERE

Welcome to a new book!

This is your book! Created just for you. Go ahead and write your name on the next page to make it yours.

We don't want you to just read this book but explore it.

Turn the page to see three ways to explore this book!

Signed,

- Joshua

THIS BOOK
BELONGS TO

three ways to explore this book

find an adult

Tell an adult that you are reading this book. Ask them to commit to discussing the questions with you after each day.

...hen we show kindness to others, we reflect the love of Jesus Christ...

how to use this book

read the day's Bible verse:
Begin by reading the selected verse together.

dive into the devotion:
Dive into the devotion inspired by the verse, exploring its meanings and applications.

discuss:
Discuss questions related to the verse and devotion, sharing insights and perspectives.

reflect:
Jot down thoughts, prayers, and reflections.

pray:
Read and connect with the prayer provided.

let's do it!

Whether you do one page a day, one page a week, or one page a month, these twenty days will help you start to understand God's design for your friendships.

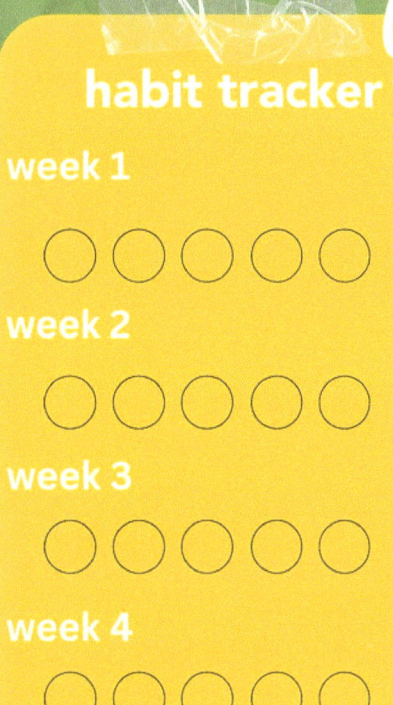

habit tracker

week 1
○ ○ ○ ○ ○

week 2
○ ○ ○ ○ ○

week 3
○ ○ ○ ○ ○

week 4
○ ○ ○ ○ ○

week 1
verses

Day 1: Be Kind to Everyone
Ephesians 4:32 (ESV)
"Be kind to one another, tenderhearted, forgiving one another, as God in Christ forgave you."

Day 2: Be Brave
Joshua 1:9 (ESV)
"Have I not commanded you? Be strong and courageous. Do not be frightened, and do not be dismayed, for the Lord your God is with you wherever you go."

Day 3: Include Others
Matthew 22:39 (ESV)
"And a second is like it:
You shall love your neighbor as yourself."

Day 4: Embrace Differences
1 Corinthians 12:12 (ESV)
"For just as the body is one and has many members, and all the members of the body, though many, are one body, so it is with Christ."

Day 5: Pray for Friendship
Philippians 4:6 (ESV)
"Do not be anxious about anything, but in everything by prayer and supplication with thanksgiving let your requests be made known to God."

making new friends

week 2

verses

Day 1: Seek Wisdom
James 1:5 (ESV)
"If any of you lacks wisdom, let him ask God, who gives generously to all without reproach, and it will be given him."

Day 2: Set Priorities
Matthew 6:33 (ESV)
"But seek first the kingdom of God and his righteousness, and all these things will be added to you."

Day 3: Resist Peer Pressure
Romans 12:2 (ESV)
"Do not be conformed to this world, but be transformed by the renewal of your mind, that by testing you may discern what is the will of God, what is good and acceptable and perfect."

Day 4: For God's Glory
1 Corinthians 10:31 (ESV)
"So, whether you eat or drink, or whatever you do, do all to the glory of God."

Day 5: Trust God's Guidance
Proverbs 3:5-6 (ESV)
"Trust in the Lord with all your heart, and do not lean on your own understanding. In all your ways acknowledge him, and he will make straight your paths."

making wise choices

Day 1: Peacekeeping
Matthew 5:9 (ESV)
"Blessed are the peacemakers,
for they shall be called sons of God."

Day 2: Listen and Understand
James 1:19 (ESV)
"Know this, my beloved brothers: let every person be quick to
hear, slow to speak, slow to anger."

Day 3: Speak Truth in Love
Ephesians 4:15 (ESV)
"Rather, speaking the truth in love, we are to grow up in every
way into him who is the head, into Christ."

Day 4: Live with Peace
Romans 12:18 (ESV)
"If possible, so far as it depends on you, live peaceably with all."

Day 5: Trust God's Peace
Philippians 4:6-7 (ESV)
"Do not be anxious about anything, but in everything by prayer
and supplication with thanksgiving let your requests be made
known to God. And the peace of God, which surpasses all
understanding, will guard your hearts and your minds in Christ
Jesus."

conflict resolution

week 4
verses

Day 1: Understand Bullying
Psalm 146:7 (ESV)
"Who executes justice for the oppressed, who gives food to the hungry. The Lord sets the prisoners free."

Day 2: Respond with Love
Luke 6:27-28 (ESV)
"But I say to you who hear, Love your enemies, do good to those who hate you, bless those who curse you, pray for those who abuse you."

Day 3: Seek Help and Support
Galatians 6:2 (ESV)
"Bear one another's burdens, and so fulfill the law of Christ."

Day 4: Forgiveness and Healing
Colossians 3:13 (ESV)
"Bear with one another and, if one has a complaint against another, forgiving each other; as the Lord has forgiven you, so you also must forgive."

Day 5: Stand Strong in Faith
Psalm 18:2 (ESV)
"The Lord is my rock and my fortress and my deliverer, my God, my rock, in whom I take refuge, my shield, and the horn of my salvation, my stronghold."

overcoming bullying

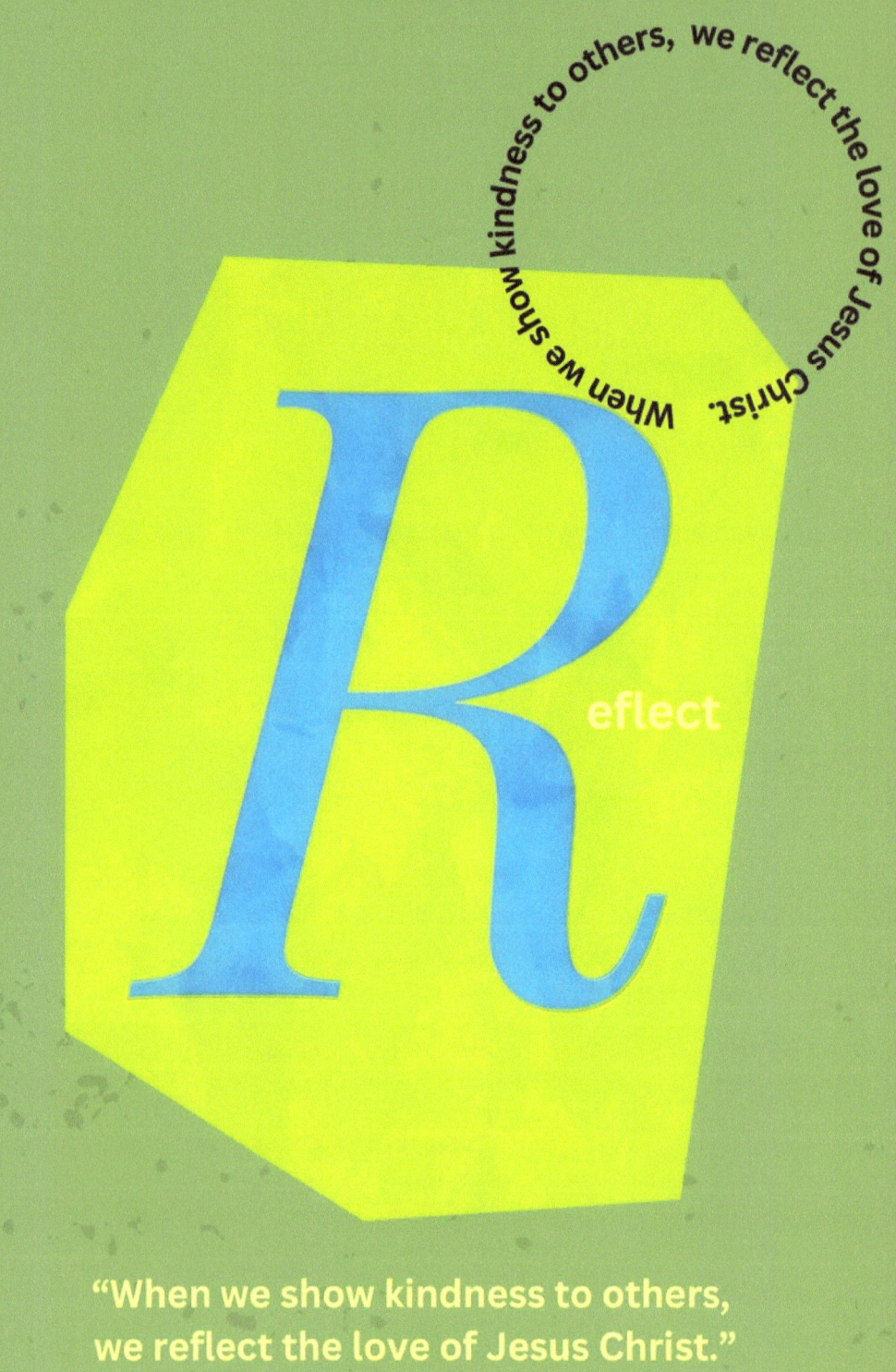

Reflect

When we show kindness to others, we reflect the love of Jesus Christ.

"When we show kindness to others, we reflect the love of Jesus Christ."

table of contents

week

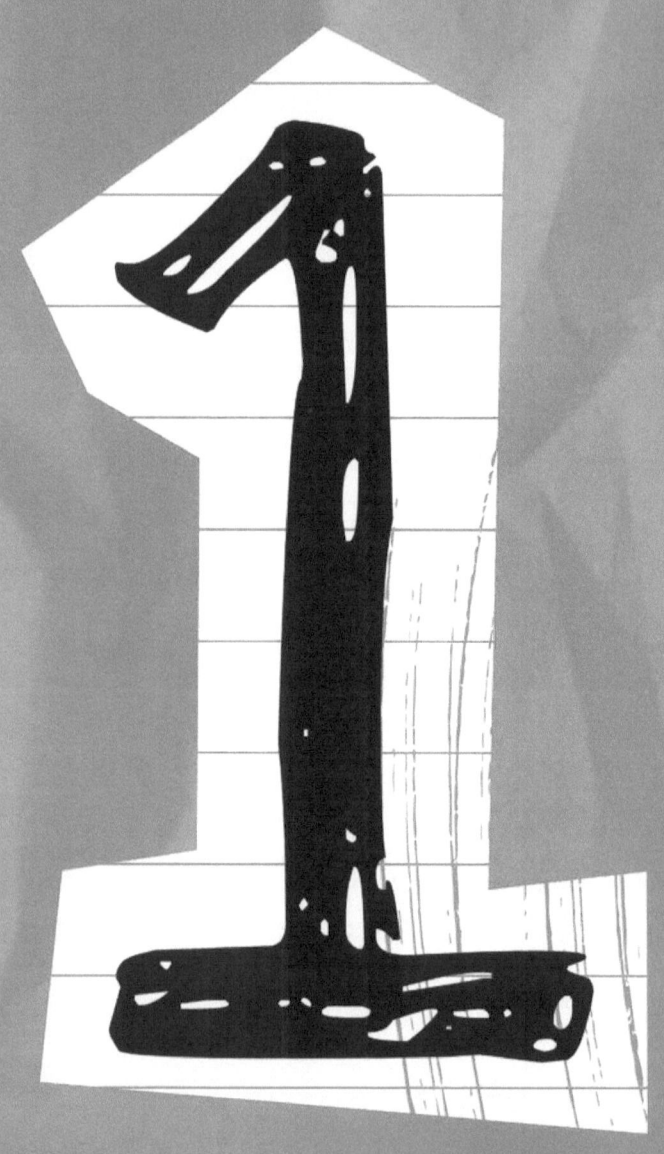

making
new
friends

making new friends

introduction

Have you ever wondered how to make more friends? This week, we're talking about exactly that! We'll learn why it's important to include everyone and be kind, and how being brave helps us make friends, too. Get ready to learn all about making friends, being brave, and spreading kindness!

overview

1. day one: be kind to everyone — **Ephesians 4:32**
2. day two: be brave — **Joshua 1:9**
3. day three: include others — **Matthew 22:39**
4. day four: embrace differences — **1 Corinthians 12:12**
5. day five: pray for friendship — **Philippians 4:6**

be kind to everyone.

Read: Ephesians 4:32

Have you ever felt really happy when someone was kind to you?

• What happened?

• How did it make you feel?

Kindness is like a bright light that shines in our hearts and makes the world better.

The book of Ephesians teaches us that kindness is not just about being nice; it's also about being compassionate and forgiving.

In Ephesians 4:32, Paul tells us to be kind, caring, and forgiving to each other. Kindness isn't just about being nice on the outside. It means really caring about others and being ready to forgive them, just like Jesus forgave us.

When we show kindness to others, we reflect the love of Jesus Christ.

Imagine: You're starting at a new school, and you don't know anyone. You're nervous, and you're not sure how to make friends. That's where kindness comes in. Showing kindness to others, especially in new situations, helps us build connections and friendships.

what's next

discussion questions

1. How can you practice kindness, compassion, and forgiveness in everyday interactions, even when it's challenging?
2. How does understanding that God forgave us impact how we forgive others?
3. Can you share when someone showed you kindness or forgiveness that made a significant difference in your life?

let's pray

Dear God, thank You for teaching us to love others just like You love us. Help us to be inclusive and reach out to those who might feel left out or lonely. Give us the courage and kindness to be a friend to everyone we meet. In Jesus' name, we pray. Amen.

be kind to everyone.

today i'm grateful for:

1. _____

2. _____

3. _____

today i learned that: _____

_____

_____

_____

my thoughts for the day: _____

_____

_____

_____

be brave.

Read: Joshua 1:9

Have you ever felt a little nervous about talking to someone new? It's okay if you have—many of us feel that way sometimes.

Joshua 1:9 reminds us that God is always with us, giving us the strength and courage we need, even when we're a bit scared.

Imagine if Joshua had been too afraid to lead the people of Israel into the Promised Land. He might have missed out on amazing blessings! But because he trusted in God and was brave, he led his people to great victories.

Similarly, when we're brave and initiate conversations with new people, we open doors to new friendships, learning opportunities, and even ways to share God's love. It might feel scary at first, but remember, God is right there cheering you on.

Here are a few tips to help you be brave and start conversations:

1. *Smile:* A smile can go a long way in making someone feel comfortable. It shows that you're friendly and approachable.

2. *Ask Questions:* People love to talk about themselves! Ask simple questions like, "What's your favorite subject in school?" or "Do you have any pets?"

3. *Listen:* Pay attention to what the other person is saying. It shows that you care about them and what they have to say.

4. *Be Yourself:* Don't try to be someone you're not. Just be genuine and let your unique personality shine through.

what's next

discussion questions

1. What are some situations where you feel nervous or hesitant to start a conversation with someone new?
2. Can you think of a time when you started a conversation with someone you didn't know very well? How did it make you feel?
3. Can you think of a time when you relied on your faith to help you be brave in a social situation?

let's pray

Dear God, thank You for teaching us to love others just like You love us. Help us to include others and reach out to those who might feel left out or lonely. Give us the courage and kindness to be a friend to everyone we meet. In Jesus' name, we pray. Amen.

be brave.

today i'm grateful for:

1. _____

2. _____

3. _____

today i learned that: _____

_____

_____

_____

my thoughts for the day: _____

_____

_____

_____

include others.

Read: Matthew 22:39

Have you ever felt left out or lonely? It doesn't feel very good, does it?

Describe how it made you feel:

But, guess what? We can make a big difference by reaching out and including those who might be feeling that way.

Matthew 22:39 says we should treat others how we want to be treated. Just imagine if everyone did that—the world would be such a happier place! Think about a time when you felt included and welcomed by others.

Maybe it was when a classmate invited you to play with them at recess or someone saved you a seat at lunch.

How did it make you feel? Probably pretty happy and appreciated, right?

Now, think about how you can be like that for someone else. Maybe a new kid in your class doesn't have anyone to sit with at lunch. Or perhaps a shy student always seems left out during group activities. You can make a difference by reaching out to them, saying hello, and including them in your games or conversations.

Here are a few ways you can include others:

1. *Say Hello*: A simple "hello" can go a long way in making someone feel noticed and welcomed.

2. *Invite Them to Join You*: Whether it's a game at recess or a group project in class, inviting someone to join shows that you care about them and want them to be included.

3. *Be Kind*: Small acts of kindness—like sharing your snacks or helping someone with their homework—can make a big difference in someone's day.

what's next

discussion questions

1. Can you think of a time when you felt included by others?
2. Why do you think it's important to include others, even if they seem different from you or you don't know them very well?
3. Can you share a time when you reached out to include someone who seemed left out or lonely?

let's pray

Dear God, thank You for teaching us to love others just like You love us. Help us to be inclusive and reach out to those who might feel left out or lonely. Give us the courage and kindness to be a friend to everyone we meet. In Jesus' name, we pray. Amen.

include others.

today i'm grateful for:

1. _____

2. _____

3. _____

today i learned that: _____

_____

_____

_____

my thoughts for the day: _____

_____

_____

_____

embrace differences.

Read: 1 Corinthians 12:12

Have you ever noticed how each person is unique in their own way? We all have different talents, interests, and backgrounds, and that's what makes the world so colorful and interesting!

List your different talents and interests:

1 Corinthians 12:12 reminds us that even though we're all different, we're all part of God's family, working together like the different parts of a body.

Think about it like this: imagine if every person in the world liked the exact same things, wore the same clothes, and had the same hobbies. Wouldn't that be boring? But because we're all unique, we can learn so much from each other and make amazing friends with people who are different from us.

Sometimes, making friends with someone who seems different can be a little scary. But that's when great things can happen! When we take the time to get to know someone different from us, we often find that we have a lot in common, too.

Here are a few tips for embracing differences and making new friends:

1. *Be Curious:* Ask questions and learn about what makes each person special. You might be surprised by what you have in common!

2. *Be Kind:* Treat others how you want to be treated, with respect and kindness, no matter how different they may seem.

3. *Look for Common Ground:* Focus on what you have in common with a new person, whether it's a favorite hobby, a love for animals, or even a shared sense of humor.

what's next

discussion questions

1. Can you think of a time when you made a new friend who seemed different from you? What did you discover that you had in common?
2. Why do you think it's important to embrace our differences and celebrate the unique qualities that make each person special?
3. How can we show kindness and respect to others, especially when they seem different from us?

let's pray

Dear God, thank You for creating each of us uniquely and wonderfully. Help us to embrace our differences and celebrate the diversity in the world around us. Give us the courage to reach out and make friends with those who are different from us, just like You would. In Jesus' name, we pray. Amen.

embrace each other's differences.

today i'm grateful for:

1. _____

2. _____

3. _____

today i learned that: _____

_____

_____

_____

my thoughts for the day: _____

_____

_____

_____

pray for friendship.

Read: Philippians 4:6

Have you ever wished for a new friend?

Someone who understands you and shares your joys and struggles? Prayer is a powerful way to invite God into our lives and ask for His guidance in all things, including friendships.

Philippians 4:6 reminds us that we can talk to God about anything, including our hopes for new friendships.

Imagine asking God to bring a new friend into your life—someone who loves to play the same games as you, laughs at your jokes, and understands you like no one else. Well, you can! God cares about every aspect of our lives, including our friendships, and He loves to hear our prayers.

How can we pray for friendship?

1. *Ask for Guidance:* Pray and ask God to guide you to the right people—those who will be kind, supportive, and encouraging friends.

2. *Pray for Open Hearts:* Ask God to open your heart and the hearts of others to new friendships, helping you connect with those who share your interests and values.

3. *Be Thankful:* Remember to thank God for the friends you already have and for the blessings of friendship in your life. Gratitude opens our hearts to even more blessings!

what's next

discussion questions

1. Why do you think prayer is important when making new friends?
2. Can you share a time when you prayed for something and felt like God answered your prayer?
3. How can we show gratitude for the friends we already have in our lives?

let's pray

Dear God, thank You for being our loving Father who cares about every aspect of our lives, including our friendships. Please guide us to new friends who will bring joy, laughter, and support into our lives. Help us to be good friends to others, showing kindness, understanding, and love. In Jesus' name, we pray. Amen.

pray for friendships.

today i'm grateful for:

1. _____

2. _____

3. _____

today i learned that: _____

_____

_____

_____

my thoughts for the day: _____

_____

_____

_____

week

making
wise
choices

week two

making wise choices

introduction

Have you ever felt unsure about making the right choices? Let's dive into how to make good decisions and trust in God.

First up, we'll learn how to ask God for wisdom. Then, we'll figure out how to put God first in everything. After that, we'll chat about standing strong against peer pressure and remembering what God says is true. Then, we'll see how everything we do can show how awesome God is.

Finally, we'll talk about trusting God to guide us. Each day, we'll discover something cool from the Bible!

overview

1. day one: seek wisdom — **James 1:5**
2. day two: set priorities — **Matthew 6:33**
3. day three: resist peer pressure — **Romans 12:2**
4. day four: for God's glory — **1 Corinthians 10:31**
5. day five: trust God's guidance — **Proverbs 3:5-6**

seek wisdom.

Read: James 1:5

As you step into the new adventures of 4th, 5th, and 6th grade, you'll encounter lots of decisions and responsibilities. But don't worry—you don't have to face them alone.

Share a time when you prayed for wisdom about something:

James 1:5 says if we need God's wisdom, we just have to ask Him for it! Isn't that amazing? God wants to give us wisdom, and He doesn't hold back. All we have to do is ask!

What is wisdom anyway?

Wisdom is like having a superpower—it helps us make good choices, understand things better, and treat others with kindness and respect. When we seek wisdom from God, we ask Him to help us see things from His perspective and make decisions that honor Him.

As you navigate the next few years, you'll face all sorts of decisions—like which friends to spend time with, how to handle challenges at school, and what activities to participate in. These decisions might seem small, but they can have a big impact on your life. That's why it's so important to seek wisdom from God in everything you do.

Here are a few ways you can seek wisdom from God:

1. *Pray:* Talk to God and ask Him for wisdom. He's always ready to listen and help you.

2. *Read the Bible:* God's Word is full of wisdom and guidance for every situation. Spend time reading the Bible and see what God has to say about the decisions you're facing.

3. *Listen to Wise Advice:* Pay attention to the advice of parents, teachers, small group leaders, and other wise adults in your life.

what's next

discussion questions

1. How do you think God's wisdom can help you with your decisions and challenges?
2. Can you share a time when you prayed for wisdom about something and felt like God helped you make a good decision?
3. How can you tell if the advice you receive from others aligns with God's wisdom?

let's pray

Dear God, thank You for being our source of wisdom and guidance. Please help us seek wisdom from You in all we do, especially as we navigate our preteen years. Give us the courage to make decisions that honor You and bless others. In Jesus' name, we pray. Amen.

seek wisdom.

notes

today i'm grateful for:

1. _____

2. _____

3. _____

today i learned that: _____

_____

_____

_____

my thoughts for the day: _____

_____

_____

_____

set priorities.

Read: Matthew 6:33

What is most important to you?

You'll always have lots of things trying to get your attention—schoolwork, friends, activities, and more. But God wants to be at the top of our priority list!

Take a second to jot down your top five priorities.

1. _____

2. _____

3. _____

4. _____

5. _____

Matthew 6:33 says that if we make God's kingdom and His ways our top priority, everything else will fall into place. How awesome is that?

So, what does it mean to seek God's kingdom first? It means putting Him at the center of everything we do—at school, at home, and with our friends. When we make decisions and manage our time, we should ask ourselves: "Is this pleasing to God? Does this align with His values?"

Let's break it down:

1. *Put God in Your Schedule:* Just like you have a schedule for school and activities, set aside time each day to spend with God—in prayer, reading the Bible, or just talking to Him.

2. *Make Wise Choices:* When faced with decisions about how to spend your time or what activities to participate in, think about whether they honor God. Choose activities and friendships that help you grow closer to Him and show His love.

3. *Trust God's Plan:* Sometimes, things don't go according to our plans, and that's okay! Trust that God has a perfect plan for your life, and seek His ways when things get tough.

what's next

discussion questions

1. Why do you think making God the top priority in our lives is important?
2. Can you share a time when you had to decide how to spend your time?
3. How can we make sure God stays at the center of our lives, even when we're busy with school, activities, and friendships?

let's pray

Dear God, thank You for being the most important priority in our lives. Help us seek Your kingdom first in all we do and make decisions that honor You. Guide us as we navigate 4th, 5th, and 6th grade, and help us to trust in Your perfect plan for our lives. In Jesus' name, we pray. Amen.

set your priorities.

notes

today i'm grateful for:

1. _____

2. _____

3. _____

today i learned that: _____

_____

_____

_____

my thoughts for the day: _____

_____

_____

_____

resist peer pressure.

Read: Romans 12:2

As you navigate school, you might encounter situations where your friends or classmates want you to do things you know aren't right. But God is on your side, giving you the strength to stand firm in your faith.

Write some things that are important for you to find in a good friend:

Romans 12:2 reminds us that we shouldn't follow along with what everyone else is doing if it goes against God's will.

How can we resist peer pressure and stand firm in our faith?

Here are a few tips:

1. *Know Your Values:* Take some time to think about what's important to you and what you believe in. When you know your values, it's easier to make decisions that honor God, even when others pressure you to do otherwise.

2. *Be Confident:* Remember that saying "no" is okay if something doesn't feel right to you. Be confident in who you are and your choices, knowing that God is pleased when we follow Him.

3. *Find Support:* Surround yourself with friends who share your values and encourage you to do what's right. Together, you can support each other and stand strong against negative influences.

what's next

discussion questions

1. Can you think of a time when you felt pressured to do something that went against your values or beliefs? How did you handle the situation?
2. How does knowing God's will help us make the right choices?
3. How can we encourage our friends to make choices that honor God?

let's pray

Dear God, thank You for giving us the strength to resist peer pressure and stand firm in our faith. Help us know Your will and make choices that honor You, even when it's hard. Give us the courage to be true to ourselves and follow Your path for our lives. In Jesus' name, we pray. Amen.

resist peer pressure.

today i'm grateful for:

1. _____

2. _____

3. _____

today i learned that: _____

_____

_____

_____

my thoughts for the day: _____

_____

_____

_____

for God's glory.

Read: 1 Corinthians 10:31

Have you ever found yourself in a situation where you had to choose between doing what you knew was right and following along with what everyone else was doing?

During the next few years, you'll have lots of opportunities to make choices—from how you spend your free time to how you treat others. But no matter what you do, you can do it all to honor God!

1 Corinthians 10:31 means that every little thing we do—whether playing Fortnite, using our cellphones, or helping out at home—can be done in a way that brings glory to God.

How can we take ownership of our actions and do everything for God's glory?

IN ALL
things
GIVE
thanks

Here are a few tips:

1. *Think Before You Act:* Before you make a choice or do something, take a moment to think about whether it's something that honors God. Ask yourself: "Is this something Jesus would want me to do?"

2. *Take Responsibility:* If you make a mistake or do something wrong, don't be afraid to admit it and take responsibility for your actions. Apologize if necessary, and try to make things right.

3. *Be a Good Example:* Show others what it looks like to live for God's glory in everything you do. Whether it's being kind to a friend, helping out around the house, or showing respect to your teachers, let your actions speak louder than words.

what's next

discussion questions

1. Can you think of a time when you had to make a choice, and you thought about whether it honored God?
2. How does your behavior reflect your love for God?
3. How can we demonstrate our love for God through our actions at home, at school, and with our friends?

let's pray

Dear God, thank You for giving us the freedom to make choices and the opportunity to honor You in everything we do. Help us to take ownership of our actions and always seek to bring glory to Your name. Help us to shine Your light wherever we go. In Jesus' name, we pray. Amen.

do it for God's glory.

today i'm grateful for:

1. _____

2. _____

3. _____

today i learned that: _____

_____

_____

_____

my thoughts for the day: _____

_____

_____

_____

trust God's guidance.

Read: Proverbs 3:5-6

Today, we're talking about something really special: trusting God's guidance.

You'll encounter many decisions and challenges. But you don't have to figure it all out on your own. God is always there, ready to guide you every step of the way.

Proverbs 3:5-6 means that when we trust God with all our hearts and seek His guidance, He will lead us on the right path.

How can we trust God's guidance in our everyday lives?

Here are a few tips:

1. *Pray:* Take time each day to talk to God and ask for His wisdom and guidance. Share your hopes, fears, and dreams with Him, and listen for His still, small voice speaking to your heart.

2. *Listen to His Word:* Spend time reading the Bible, God's Word. It's like a map that shows us the right way to go. Look for verses that speak to your situation, and let God's truth guide your decisions.

3. *Obey His Voice:* When you sense God prompting you to do something or guiding you in a certain direction, obey Him. Trust that He knows what's best for you, even if it's not what you expected.

what's next

discussion questions

1. Can you share a time when you felt like God was guiding you about a decision or situation?
2. Why do you think it's important to trust God's guidance, even when it might not match what we originally planned or expected?
3. How can we remind ourselves to lean on God's understanding rather than relying on our own?

let's pray

Dear God, thank You for always being there for us and guiding us on the right path. Help us to trust You with all our hearts and seek Your guidance in all things. Give us the courage to obey Your voice and follow where You lead us. In Jesus' name, we pray. Amen.

trust

God's guidance.

notes

today i'm grateful for:

1. _____

2. _____

3. _____

today i learned that: _____

_____

_____

_____

my thoughts for the day: _____

_____

_____

_____

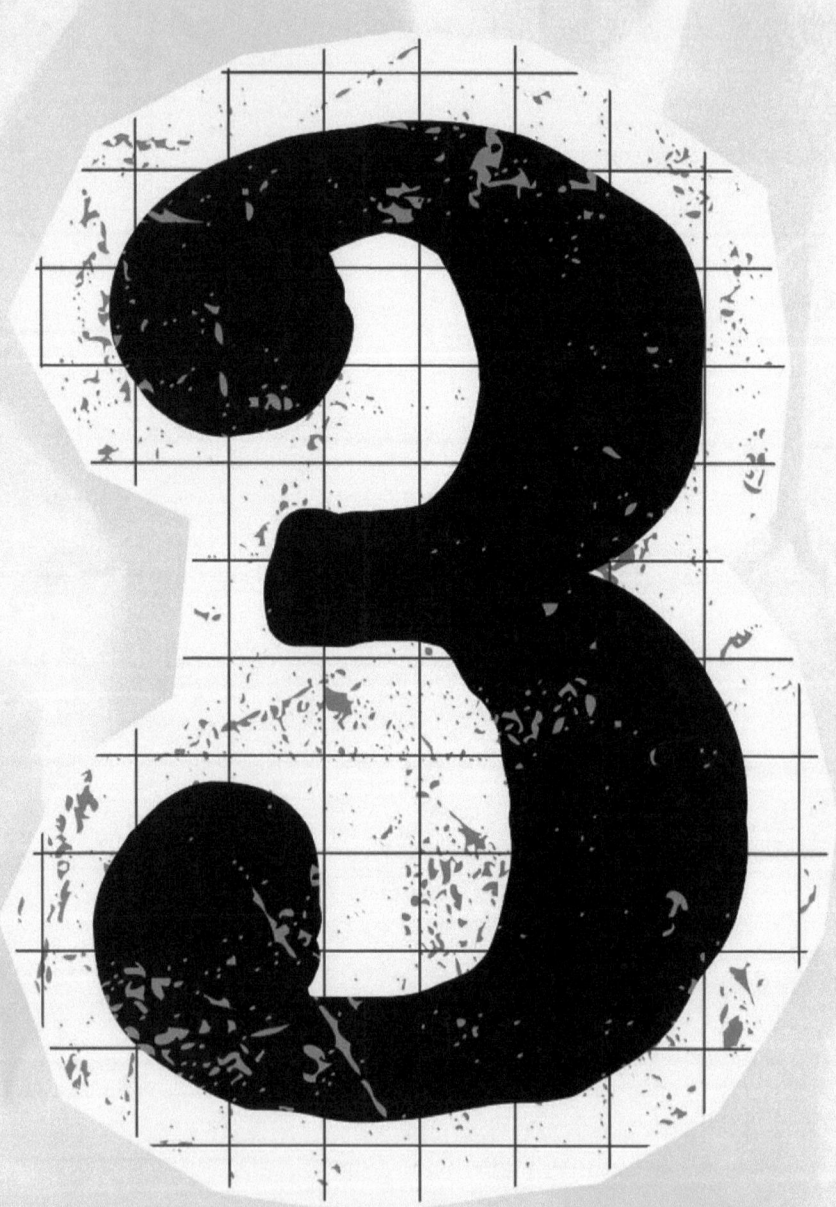

week

conflict
resolution

conflict resolution

introduction

Have you ever wondered how we can have more peace in our lives, especially when there's conflict? We'll use Bible verses to help us understand how to keep peace with others, even when things get tough.

First, we'll learn about making peace, just like Jesus said. Then, we'll find out why listening and understanding are so important in resolving conflicts. After that, we'll talk about telling the truth in a nice way, which helps us keep the peace. Next, we'll see why living peacefully is super cool, especially when we're facing disagreements.

Finally, we'll discover how we can trust God to give us peace when we feel worried or scared during conflicts.

overview

1. day one: peacekeeping — **Matthew 5:9**
2. day two: listen & understand — **James 1:19**
3. day three: speak truth in love — **Ephesians 4:15**
4. day four: live with peace — **Romans 12:18**
5. day five: trust God's peace — **Philippians 4:6-7**

peacekeeping.

Read: Matthew 5:9

Have you ever been in a situation where there was tension or disagreement?

How did that make you feel?

It's not always easy, but being a peacemaker—someone who helps bring peace—is something God smiles upon.

Matthew 5:9 says peacemakers will be called sons of God. Isn't that cool? God loves it when we spread peace and work to resolve conflicts peacefully.

It's like shining a light in a dark room—it makes everything brighter and better!

How can we be peacemakers in our everyday lives?

Here are a few tips:

1. *Listen:* When there's a disagreement or conflict, take time to listen to the other person's point of view. Listening shows that you care about their feelings and helps you understand where they're coming from.

2. *Use Kind Words:* Speak gently and respectfully, even if you disagree with someone. Kind words have the power to calm tempers and heal hurt feelings.

3. *Find Solutions:* Instead of focusing on who's right or wrong, work together to find a solution everyone can agree on.

what's next

discussion questions

1. Can you think of a time when you had to be a peacemaker with friends, family, or classmates?
2. Why do you think it's important to listen to others and speak kindly, especially when we disagree or face conflicts?
3. How can we practice spreading peace and resolving conflicts peacefully at home or school?

let's pray

Dear God, thank You for being the ultimate Peacemaker and for teaching us to spread peace wherever we go. Help us to be peacemakers in our families, schools, and communities, and resolve conflicts peacefully. Give us the courage to listen, speak kindly, and find solutions that honor You. In Jesus' name, we pray. Amen.

make peace.

today i'm grateful for:

1. _____

2. _____

3. _____

today i learned that: _____

_____

_____

_____

my thoughts for the day: _____

_____

_____

_____

listen & understand.

Read: James 1:19

Have you ever felt like nobody was listening to you? It doesn't feel good, does it? That's why it's so important to be good listeners ourselves!

What are some things that bother you?

[ ]

God wants us to be quick to listen and slow to speak—to pay attention to what others are saying before we respond.

How can we practice active listening and understanding others' perspectives?

Here are a few tips:

1. *Give Your Full Attention:* When someone is talking to you, put down any distractions—like toys or electronic devices— and give them your full attention. Look them in the eye and show them that you're listening.

2. *Ask Questions:* If you're not sure what someone means or want to learn more about their perspective, ask questions! Asking questions shows that you care about what they're saying and helps you understand them better.

3. *Empathize:* Put yourself in the other person's shoes and try to see things from their point of view. Even if you don't agree with them, showing empathy and understanding can help resolve conflicts and strengthen relationships.

what's next

discussion questions

1. Can you share a time when you felt like someone really listened to you and understood how you were feeling?
2. Why do you think it's important to be quick to listen and slow to speak, as the Bible verse says?
3. Can you think of a situation where you had to put yourself in someone else's shoes to better understand their point of view?

let's pray

Dear God, thank You for teaching us the importance of listening and understanding others. Help us to be quick to listen, slow to speak, and slow to become angry. Give us the wisdom and empathy to see things from others' perspectives and resolve conflicts peacefully. In Jesus' name, we pray. Amen.

listen to understand.

today i'm grateful for:

1. _____

2. _____

3. _____

today i learned that: _____

_____

_____

_____

my thoughts for the day: _____

_____

_____

_____

speak truth in love.

Read: Ephesians 4:15

Have you ever had to tell someone something they might not want to hear?

How did they respond?

It can be hard, but speaking truthfully and with love can lead to greater understanding and stronger relationships.

When we speak the truth in love, we become more like Jesus and help build up the body of Christ—that's us, God's family!

How can we speak truth in love when addressing conflicts or confronting issues?

Here are a few tips:

1. *Be Honest:* Always tell the truth, even if it's difficult. Honesty is the foundation of trust, and it's important to be truthful with others, whether it's your parents, teachers, small group leaders, or friends.

2. *Use Kind Words:* Speak gently and respectfully, even when discussing something challenging. Kind words can soften the blow and show that you care about the other person's feelings.

3. *Focus on Solutions:* Instead of just pointing out problems, work together to find solutions. When we approach conflicts with a mindset of love and cooperation, we can often find a resolution more easily.

what's next

discussion questions

1. Can you think of a time when you had to speak truthfully to someone, even though it was difficult?
2. How do honesty and kindness strengthen our relationships with others, whether it's with parents, teachers, small group leaders, or friends?
3. How can we approach difficult conversations with kindness and respect while still being honest and truthful?

let's pray

Dear God, thank You for teaching us the importance of speaking truth in love. Help us be honest and kind in all our interactions, whether it's with our parents, teachers, small group leaders, or friends. Give us the courage to address conflicts respectfully and work towards solutions that honor You. In Jesus' name, we pray. Amen.

speak truth in love.

today i'm grateful for:

1. _____

2. _____

3. _____

today i learned that: _____

_____

_____

_____

my thoughts for the day: _____

_____

_____

_____

live with peace.

Read: Romans 12:18

Have you ever had an argument or disagreement with a friend? It's not fun, but did you know God wants us to make things right and live at peace with everyone?

God wants us to do everything we can to live in peace and harmony with others, including our friends, classmates, and even siblings!

Remember, sometimes, saying sorry and making up with someone can be hard, but it's really important and can make things better. When we make peace with others, we follow God's example and spread His love to those around us.

How can we make up with someone when conflicts arise?

Here are a few tips:

1. *Apologize:* If you've done something wrong or hurt someone's feelings, be quick to apologize. Saying sorry shows that you care about the other person's feelings and want to make things right.

2. *Listen:* Take time to listen to the other person's perspective and try to understand where they're coming from. Listening shows that you value their feelings and can help you find common ground.

3. *Find Solutions:* Instead of figuring out who's right or wrong, focus on finding solutions that work for everyone. Working together to solve problems builds trust and strengthens relationships.

what's next

discussion questions

1. Can you think of a time when you disagreed with a friend or sibling? What did you learn from the experience?
2. How does making peace with others reflect God's love and teachings?
3. How can we show humility and apologize sincerely when we've done something wrong?

let's pray

Dear God, thank You for teaching us the importance of trying to make things right. Help us to live at peace with everyone, especially our friends and classmates. Give us the courage to apologize when we've done something wrong and work towards solutions that honor You. In Jesus' name, we pray. Amen.

live with peace.

today i'm grateful for:

1. _____

2. _____

3. _____

today i learned that: _____

_____

_____

_____

my thoughts for the day: _____

_____

_____

_____

trust God's peace.

Read: Philippians 4:6-7

Have you ever felt worried or anxious about something? It's a tough feeling, but God offers us a special kind of peace—a peace that goes beyond our understanding.

When we pray and give our worries to God, He gives us His peace—a peace that's unlike anything we've ever experienced.

How can we trust God's peace, especially when we're facing conflicts or challenges?

Here are a few tips:

1. *Pray:* Take time to pray and talk to God about your worries and concerns. Tell Him what's on your heart and ask Him to give you His peace. Remember, God is always listening and cares about what you're going through.

2. *Trust God's Plan:* Even when things seem uncertain or difficult, trust that God has a plan for your life. His ways are higher than ours, and He knows what's best for us, even when we can't see it.

3. *Focus on Gratitude:* Instead of thinking about your worries, focus on things you're thankful for. When we have a heart of gratitude, it's easier to trust God and experience His peace in our lives.

what's next

discussion questions

1. Can you think of a time when you felt worried or anxious about something?
2. How does knowing that God is with us and offers us His peace help us navigate difficult situations?
3. How can we practice giving our worries to God and trusting in His plan in our everyday lives?

let's pray

Dear God, thank You for offering us Your peace, even in the midst of conflict and challenges. Help us to trust You with all our hearts and give our worries to You in prayer. May Your peace guard our hearts and minds and help us to experience the fullness of Your love. In Jesus' name, we pray. Amen.

trust God's peace.

today i'm grateful for:

1. _____

2. _____

3. _____

today i learned that: _____

_____

_____

_____

my thoughts for the day: _____

_____

_____

_____

week 4

overcoming
bullying

week four

overcoming bullying

introduction

Have you ever wondered how to deal with bullying while keeping your cool? We'll learn from stories in the Bible how to handle tough situations with grace and courage.

First, we'll understand what bullying is and how God can help us through it. Then, we'll see how responding with love, just like Jesus taught us, can make a big difference. After that, we'll talk about asking for help from trusted people and our small group leaders when we need it.

Finally, we'll find out how feeling strong and safe with God's help can help us stand tall.

overview

1. day one: understand bullying — **Psalm 146:7**
2. day two: respond with love — **Luke 6:27-28**
3. day three: seek help & support — **Galatians 6:2**
4. day four: forgiveness & healing — **Colossians 3:13**
5. day five: stand strong in faith — **Psalms 18:2**

understand bullying.

Read: Psalm 146:7

Have you ever seen or experienced bullying? It's not okay, and God cares about those who are hurt or treated unfairly.

God stands up for those who are treated unfairly or oppressed —that means He's on the side of anyone being bullied.

What is bullying? Bullying is when someone hurts, frightens, or makes fun of another person on purpose, again and again. It could be through mean words, hitting, excluding others, or spreading rumors. Bullying goes against God's love and His desire for justice and fairness.

God wants us to treat others with kindness and respect, just like He does. He wants us to stand up for those being bullied and be a friend to those who need one.

When we do that, we spread God's love and make the world a better place.

Take a moment today to think about how you can stand against bullying and show kindness to others. Whether it's being a friend to someone lonely or speaking up when you see someone being bullied, you can make a difference!

what's next

discussion questions

1. How do you think bullying goes against God's love and desire for justice?
2. Have you ever witnessed someone being bullied or experienced it yourself? How did it make you feel?
3. How can we practice showing kindness and standing up for others in our everyday lives, even when it's not easy?

let's pray

Dear God, thank You for caring about each and every one of us, especially those who are hurt or treated unfairly. Help us to stand against bullying and show kindness and love to everyone we meet. Give us the courage to speak up for those who need our help and be a friend to those who are hurting. In Jesus' name, we pray. Amen.

it's not okay to bully.

today i'm grateful for:

1. _____

2. _____

3. _____

today i learned that: _____

_____

_____

_____

my thoughts for the day: _____

_____

_____

_____

respond with love.

Read: Luke 6:27-28

Have you ever faced a situation where someone was unkind or treated you unfairly?

CIRCLE ONE: YES OR NO

It's tough, but Jesus teaches us to respond with love, even to those who mistreat us.

Jesus tells us to respond to unkindness with kindness, to hate with love, and to pray for those who mistreat us.

How can we respond to bullying or unkindness with love and compassion?

Here are a few tips:

1. *Stay Calm:* When someone is unkind or mistreats us, it's natural to feel upset or angry. But, instead of reacting with anger, try to stay calm and composed. Let an adult know what is going on. Take a deep breath and remember Jesus' words to respond with love.

2. *Show Kindness:* Even when it's hard, show kindness to those who are unkind to you. Smile, say something nice, or offer to help them. Sometimes, showing kindness can break down walls and soften hearts.

3. *Pray for Them:* Take time to pray for those who mistreat you. Ask God to bless them and help them see the importance of treating others with kindness and respect. Prayer is powerful and can bring positive change.

what's next

discussion questions

1. Can you share a time when you responded to unkindness with love or kindness?
2. How did it feel to show love to someone who mistreated you, and what was the outcome?
3. How can we show love to those who mistreat us or others?

let's pray

Dear God, thank You for teaching us to respond to unkindness with love and compassion. Help us to show kindness to those who mistreat us and pray for them. Give us the strength to follow Jesus' example and spread love wherever we go. In Jesus' name, we pray. Amen.

respond with love.

notes

today i'm grateful for:

1. _____

2. _____

3. _____

today i learned that: _____

_____

_____

_____

my thoughts for the day: _____

_____

_____

_____

seek help & support.

Read: Galatians 6:2

Have you ever faced a situation where you didn't know what to do or felt overwhelmed?

How did you respond?

It's okay to ask for help. God wants us to support each other and share our burdens. God calls us to help and support each other, just like a team working together to achieve a goal.

How can we seek help and support when we're facing bullying or difficult situations?

Here are a few tips:

1. *Talk to Trusted Adults:* If you're experiencing bullying or feeling overwhelmed, talk to a trusted adult—like a parent, teacher, or small group leader. They care about you and want to help you navigate tough times.

2. *Reach Out to Friends:* Don't be afraid to reach out to friends for support. True friends will listen to you, offer encouragement, and stand by your side during difficult times.

3. *Pray for Strength:* Take time to pray and ask God for strength and guidance. He's always there to listen to you and help you through any situation you're facing.

what's next

discussion questions

1. Can you think of a time when you needed help or support from someone you trusted?
2. Why do you think it's important to seek help from trusted adults and friends when facing bullying or difficult situations?
3. How can we encourage each other to seek help when needed and be there for one another during tough times?

let's pray

Dear God, thank You for giving us friends, family, and leaders who care about and want to support us. Help us have the courage to reach out for help when we need it and be there for others who are struggling. Give us strength and comfort as we face difficult situations, knowing that You are always with us. In Jesus' name, we pray. Amen.

find help and support.

today i'm grateful for:

1. _____

2. _____

3. _____

today i learned that: _____

_____

_____

_____

my thoughts for the day: _____

_____

_____

_____

forgiveness & healing.

Read: Colossians 3:13

Have you ever felt hurt or upset because someone was unkind to you? It's tough, but forgiveness has the power to heal our hearts and set us free.

What is forgiveness, and how does it help us heal from the hurt bullying causes?

Forgiveness is a promise not to keep a record of wrongs against someone who has hurt us. When we forgive, we're not saying that what they did was okay—we're choosing to release the hold hurt has on our hearts and move forward with love.

Forgiveness doesn't mean we forget what happened or have to be best friends with the person who hurt us. It means we let go of bitterness and seek healing for ourselves.

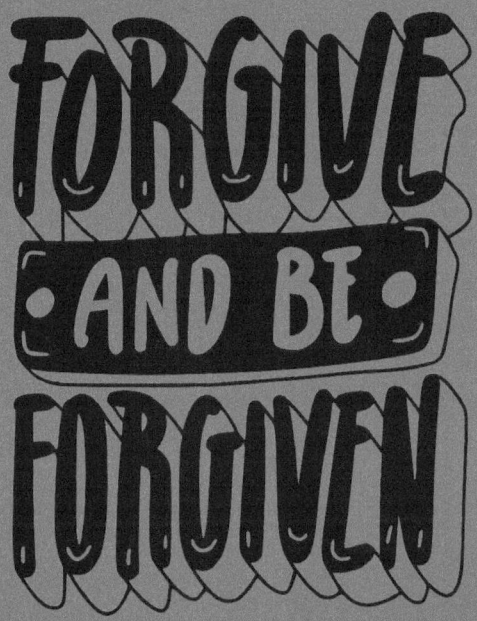

When we forgive, we free ourselves from the burden of carrying anger and resentment, and we open our hearts to God's love and healing.

Take a moment today to think about someone who has hurt you, and consider how forgiveness could bring healing to your heart. Remember, forgiveness is a journey, and it's okay to take your time and seek support from trusted adults and friends along the way.

what's next

discussion questions

1. Can you think of a time when you forgave someone who hurt you?
2. What positive changes did you notice in yourself or your relationship with that person?
3. How can we practice forgiveness in our everyday lives, even when it's challenging?

let's pray

Dear God, thank You for the gift of forgiveness and the healing it brings to our hearts. Help us to forgive those who have hurt us, just as You have forgiven us. Give us the strength and courage to let go of anger and bitterness and embrace the peace that comes from forgiveness. In Jesus' name, we pray. Amen.

forgive.

today i'm grateful for:

1. _____

2. _____

3. _____

today i learned that: _____

_____

_____

_____

my thoughts for the day: _____

_____

_____

_____

stand strong in faith.

Read: Psalms 18:2

Have you ever faced a challenge or felt scared or alone?

List some things you're afraid of:

It's okay because we have a source of strength that never fails: God. God is like a mighty fortress, always there to protect us and give us strength.

How can we stand strong in faith when facing challenges like bullying?

Here are a few tips:

1. *Pray:* Take time to pray and talk to God about your fears and worries. He's always listening, and He promises to be with us no matter what we're facing.

2. *Remember God's Promises:* God promises to never leave us or forsake us. He is our rock, refuge, and source of strength and protection. When we remember His promises, we can face challenges with confidence and courage.

3. *Lean on Others:* Don't be afraid to lean on others for support—whether it's your family, friends, or small group leaders. God has placed people in your life to help and encourage you when you need it most.

what's next

discussion questions

1. Can you share a time when you felt scared or alone, but you found strength in God's presence? How did God help you through that challenging situation?
2. How does knowing God is our rock and fortress give us courage and confidence?
3. How can we remind ourselves of God's promises and rely on His strength to face challenges with courage and confidence?

let's pray

Dear God, thank You for being our rock, our fortress, and our source of strength and protection. Help us to stand strong in faith, trusting in Your promises and leaning on You for strength. Give us courage and confidence to face any challenge that comes our way, knowing that You are always with us. Amen.

stand strong in faith.

today i'm grateful for:

1. _____

2. _____

3. _____

today i learned that: _____

_____

_____

_____

my thoughts for the day: _____

_____

_____

_____

conclusion

conclusion

As we wrap up our journey together, it's amazing to reflect on all we've discovered over these weeks.

WEEK ONE showed us how a simple act of kindness or a brave step toward including others can spark beautiful friendships that make our lives better.

WEEK TWO challenged us to trust in God's wisdom and prioritize His guidance in every decision we make.

WEEK THREE explored the significance of peace in our relationships, even when we have conflicts.

WEEK FOUR confronted the difficult topic of bullying and taught us how to respond with grace and courage, just as Jesus did.

We may not have answered all of your questions.

We may not have solved all of your problems.

But we hope that we have given you insights, practical advice, and biblical teachings to empower you to start to navigate these upcoming challenges a little more effectively.

So, this week...

Be kind.
Trust in God's wisdom.
Make peace.
Don't bully.

And remember, when we show kindness to others, we reflect the love of Jesus!

author bio

JOSHUA CELESTIN gives leadership to 4th & 5th graders at First Orlando, which means he spends every day thinking about, speaking to, interacting with, and playing games with preteens, as well as recruiting leaders to work with them.

Before stepping into his current role, Josh spent five years as a filmmaker and is an Emmy award-winning cinematographer, dedicated to telling and sharing others' stories.

Josh did not limit himself to storytelling through film but extended his talents to Christian hip-hop as well.

Most importantly, Josh leads a small group of 5th graders every Sunday. If you want to be Josh's best friend, just buy him a pizza.

For more resources check out . . .

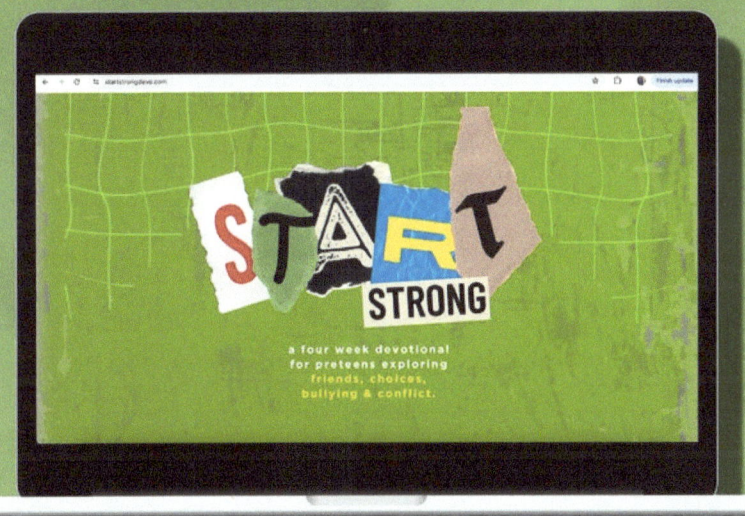

Dive into weekly content, and get practical tips in our Parent Corner. Start today and deepen your faith in a whole new way!

STARTSTRONGDEVO.COM